A Note to Parents and Teachers

DK READERS is a compelling reading programme for children, designed in conjunction with leading literacy experts, including Cliff Moon M.Ed., Honorary Fellow of the University of Reading. Cliff Moon has spent many years as a teacher and teacher educator specializing in reading and has written more than 140 books for children and teachers. He reviews regularly for teachers' journals.

Beautiful illustrations and superb full-colour photographs combine with engaging, easy-to-read stories to offer a fresh approach to each subject in the series. Each DK READER is guaranteed to capture a child's interest while developing his or her reading skills, general knowledge, and love of reading.

The five levels of DK READERS are aimed at different reading abilities, enabling you to choose the books that are exactly right for your child:

Pre-level 1: Learning to read
Level 1: Beginning to read
Level 2: Beginning to read alone
Level 3: Reading alone
Level 4: Proficient readers

The "normal" age at which a child begins to read can be anywhere from three to eight years old, so these levels are only a general guideline.

No matter which level you select, you can be sure that you are helping your child learn to read, then read

DK

LONDON, NEW YORK, MUNICH,
MELBOURNE and DELHI

Series Editor Penny Smith
Senior Art Editor Sonia Moore
DTP Designer Almudena Díaz
Production Angela Graef
Photographer Andy Crawford

Reading Consultant
Cliff Moon, M.Ed.

Published in Great Britain by
Dorling Kindersley Limited
80 Strand, London WC2R ORL

2 4 6 8 10 9 7 5 3

A Penguin Company

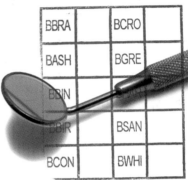

A CIP record for this book is available
from the British Library

ISBN-13: 978-1-4053-1388-9

Colour reproduction by Colourscan, Singapore
Printed and bound in China by L Rex Printing Co., Ltd.

With thanks to: The Hill View Dental Practice, Harrow, London,
for premises and staff appearing in the photographs; Cameron and Nikhita
Jackson and their mother Geeta Nanda for appearing in the photographs.
Alexander Workwear, London, for dental coats; LydiaUniforms.com for
dental scrubs; OpenWide.com for dental accessories.

All images © Dorling Kindersley
For more information see: www.dkimages.com

Discover more at
www.dk.com

DK READERS

BEGINNING
TO READ
1

A Trip to the Dentist

Written by Penny Smith

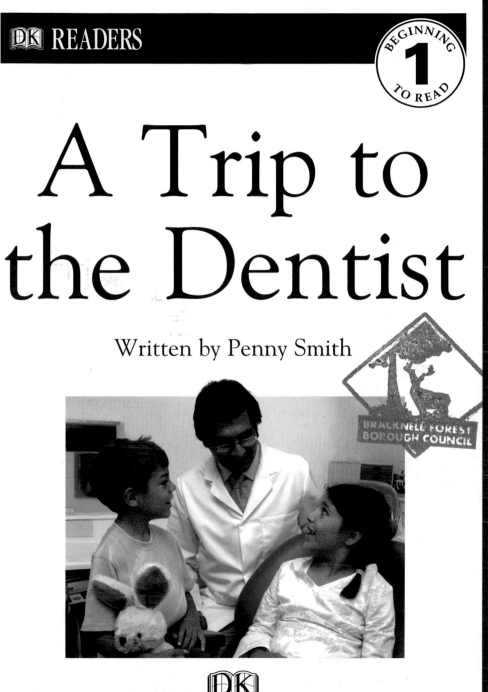

DK

A Dorling Kindersley Book

"Come on, get your coats,"
called Mum.
Sarah and her brother, Josh,
came into the room.

"It's time to go
to the dentist
for your check-ups,"
said Mum.

Soon they arrived
at the dentist's.
Mum told
the receptionist
their names.

"I want my teeth
to stay strong and
white like Rabbit's,"
Josh told her.

rabbit

7

The children played in
the waiting room until it was
time for their check-ups.

Then the dentist
took them into his room.
"Hello," he said.
"My name is Dr Richards."

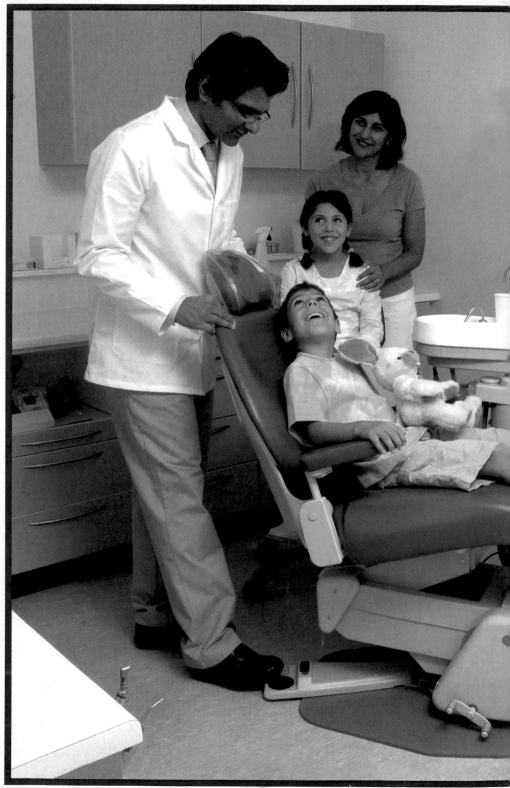

"Who's going first?"
asked Dr Richards.
Josh climbed into the chair
with Rabbit.
The dentist pressed a button
and the chair tipped
slowly backwards.

dentist

"Open wide," said Dr Richards.
First he checked Josh's gums.

Then he used a small mirror
to look for holes called cavities
in Josh's teeth.
He didn't find any cavities.

mirror

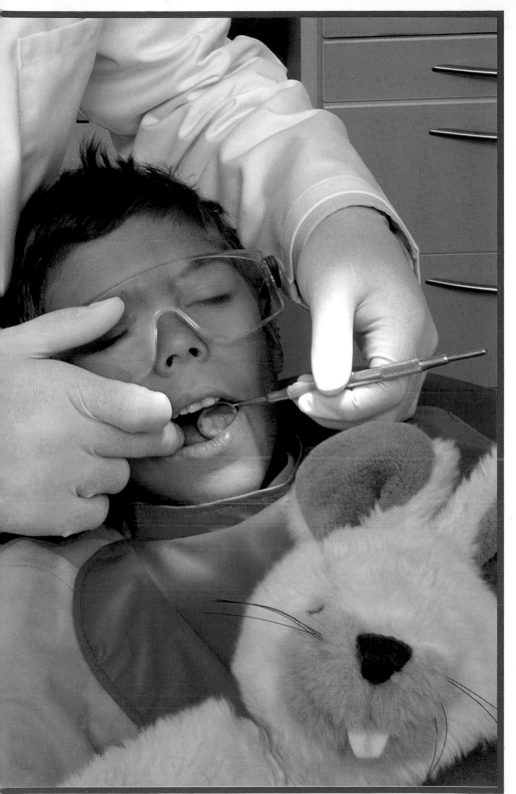

"You need to take extra care of the molars at the back of your mouth," he said. "At the moment there is a sticky layer on them. It's called plaque and it can cause cavities, so you need to brush it away."

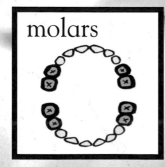

molars

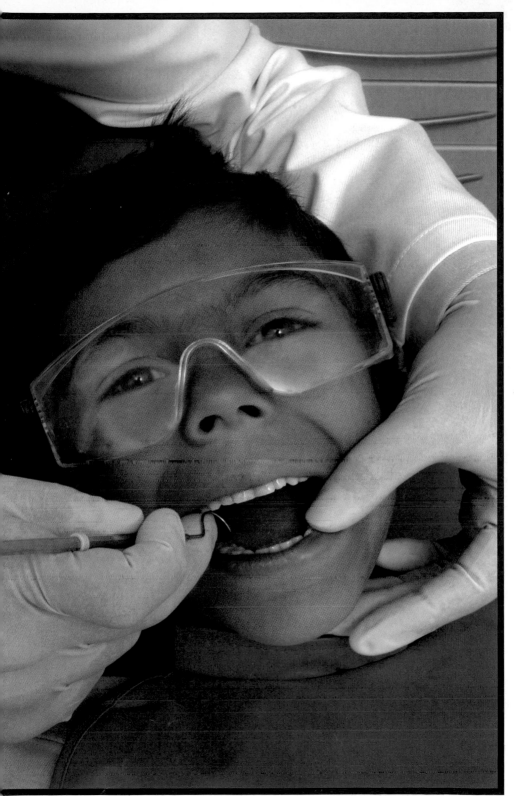

Dr Richards showed Josh
a good way to brush.

toothbrush

"Squeeze a pea-sized
blob of toothpaste
onto your toothbrush.
Then gently brush
in little circles," he said.

Josh tried brushing Rabbit's teeth. "How often do you brush your teeth?" asked Dr Richards.

"Every day, I think," said Josh. "You should brush twice a day – once in the morning and once before you go to bed," said Dr Richards.

incisors

Then it was
Sarah's turn.
"You've lost six
of your baby teeth,"
said Dr Richards.

"New incisors are growing at the front. Soon your other baby teeth will get wobbly and fall out. You'll have 32 new teeth altogether."

Then Dr Richards
found a little cavity
in one of Sarah's teeth.

"I'm going to put
a filling here," he said.
"A filling is a kind of
paste that dries hard.
It will stop the cavity
getting bigger and
giving you toothache."

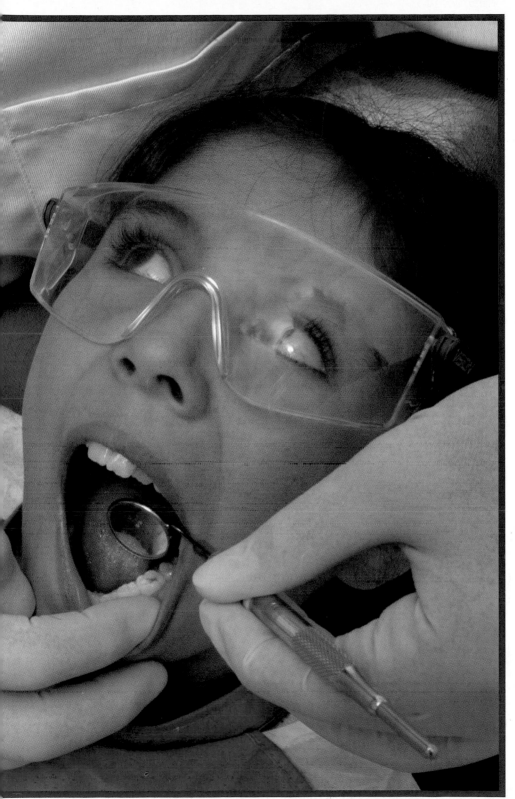

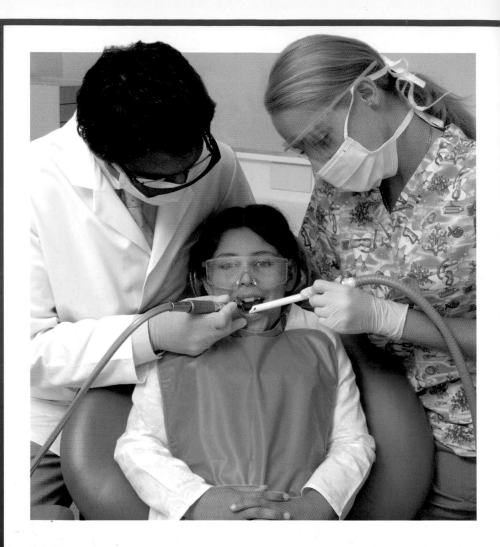

First Dr Richards cleaned
out the cavity using a drill.
His assistant, Carol, used
a suction tip to suck out
any saliva, or spit.

Then she gave Sarah
a cup of water to
rinse out her mouth.

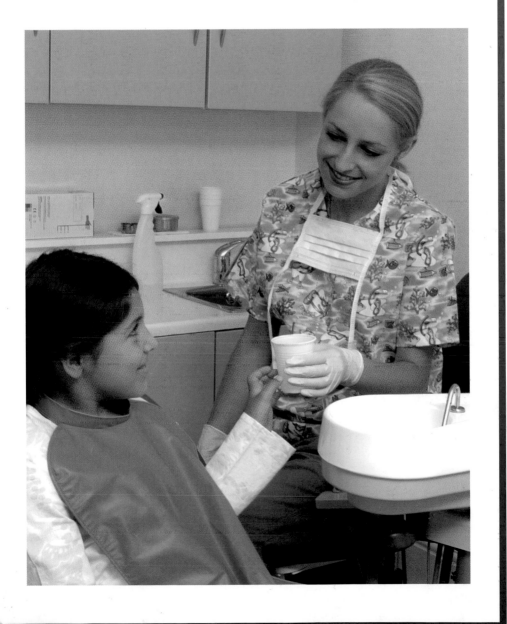

Next Dr Richards
used an air jet to
blow air into
the cavity.
This dried the
cavity so the
filling would stick.

Then he pushed the filling
neatly into the cavity.
"All done," he said.

Then Dr Richards
pointed to a chart.
It helped explain how
to prevent cavities.
"Make sure you don't
have sugary drinks
or sweets very often,
and brush your teeth
twice a day,"
he said.

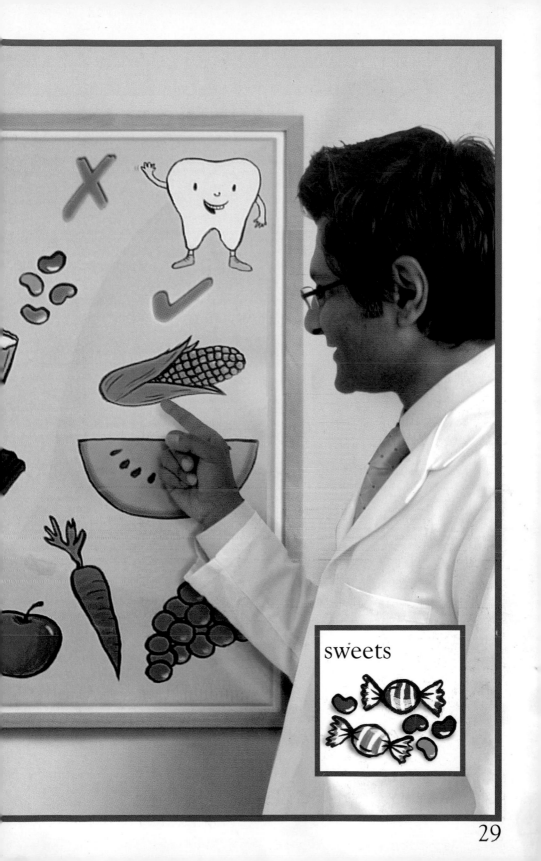

sweets

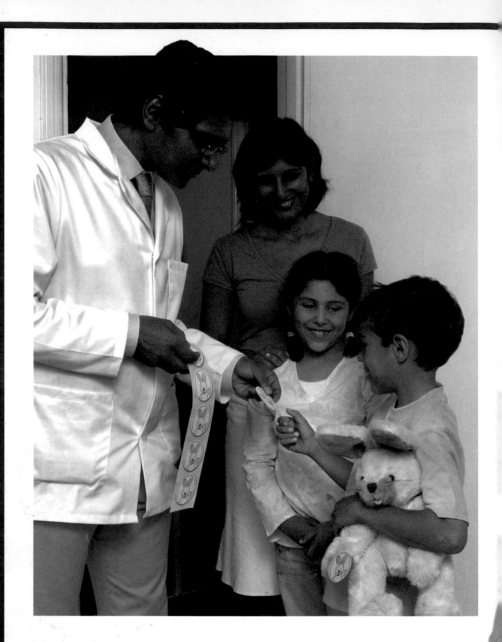

As they were leaving,
Dr Richards gave each child
a sticker of a smiling rabbit.

The sticker said,
"To keep your teeth
sparkling clean and bright,
brush early in the morning
and last thing at night."
And that's exactly what
they did!

Picture word list

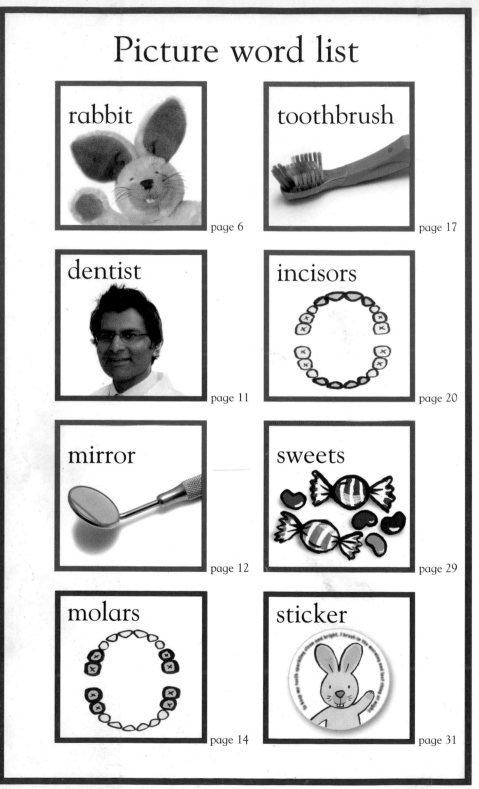

rabbit

page 6

toothbrush

page 17

dentist

page 11

incisors

page 20

mirror

page 12

sweets

page 29

molars

page 14

sticker

page 31